How I Got Into a Top-Ten Business School by Kaine T. Alozie 1

Kaine T. Alozie

HOW I GOT INTO A TOP-TEN BUSINESS SCHOOL

Cover by Effiong K. Dampha

CONTENTS

INTRODUCTION

According to BusinessWeek's 2004 rankings, these are the top-ten business schools:

Ranking	School
1	Northwestern (Kellogg)
2	Chicago
3	Pennsylvania (Wharton)
4	Stanford
5	Harvard
6	Michigan (Ross)
7	Cornell (Johnson)
8	Columbia
9	MIT (Sloan)
10	Dartmouth (Tuck)

After completing my undergraduate education in business, I knew that one day I would return to school for an MBA. Early in the game, I decided to pursue the degree from a top-ten school. An MBA from a top school seemed to have a lot to offer personally as well as professionally. It was an avenue to increase my business acumen and professional skills, and to gain access to an invaluable network of colleagues. While it seemed like the ideal environment to enhance my career, I also knew it as an intimidating and exclusive environment. Nevertheless, it became my goal to attend such an institution, although I initially had no clue as to how to accomplish that.

Then one day, I had a phone conversation with an old friend who informed me that he was resigning his position at his firm to go back to school. "Where will you be attending school?" I asked. He, without an ounce of cockiness, replied, "Harvard." Naturally impressed, I asked him some questions in order to learn from his experiences. We covered a lot of ground- from the GMAT, to letters of recommendation and financial aid. Speaking with him helped demystify the business school admissions process a little.

Previously, I thought that an expensive course was necessary to do well on the GMAT, until he told me that he self-studied for the exam. "If he could do that, why couldn't I?" I thought. When it was time to study for the exam, I bought a few different prep books and self-studied for a little over two months. I got a 730 on my first try. The cost of attendance was also an issue. How could I afford a $100,000 investment? He told me not to be overly concerned, because all students admitted into the Harvard Business School were guaranteed some form of financial aid. After having my questions answered, and after seeing this done by one of my peers, there was no question in my mind that I could accomplish this as well.

Every year, the top business schools receive hundreds of thousands of applications for admission. Offers are extended to a small percentage. Acceptance rates at the top schools can range from as low as nine percent to fifteen percent. With so many applicants to choose from, many qualified applicants are denied admission. So just what are the top business schools looking for? What qualities differentiate candidates from one another? Knowing the answer to this question early in the admissions process will not only save you time and heartache, but will also enable you to craft a more compelling application.

Using this book as a medium, I hope to do for you what my friend did for me- only on a much more detailed level. This book will serve as your guide to the business school admissions process. It will tell you what you need to do to get into a top-ten business school. We will cover topics such as the GMAT, work experience, letters of recommendation, essays, financial aid and interviews.

Two things differentiate this book from others of its kind. First, I was actually accepted to top-ten business schools- Dartmouth and Michigan. I ended up attending

Michigan with a full ride. Second, as you read through each topic in this book, you will learn how I approached it, and what worked for me. I will share with you how I studied for the GMAT, how I approached the admissions essays, and the like. In sharing this information, I must include this disclaimer: there is no "one size fits all" approach to the applications process. What worked for me may or may not work for you. I include my experiences so that you can see an approach to each of the items we will review in this text. So please, view my experiences as an example of what to do, and not as a sure-fire method of going about this process. For many, it helps to read about the experiences of others, so that they can develop a game plan of their own. I hope that this is how you will use this book.

Acceptance to a top-ten school is extremely competitive, so take every aspect of it seriously. No matter your qualifications, never come across as overconfident or cocky in your essays or during the interview. There is no such thing as a "shoe-in" when it comes to getting into business school. Many applicants with GMAT scores over 700 are turned away from top programs. Every part of the application is important, so resist the temptation to rush through any of it.

Last of all, I want to wish you good luck throughout the admissions process. It will be a very grueling but rewarding endeavor. There is a reason hundreds of thousands of applicants apply to business school every year. It's because an MBA is, perhaps, the most valuable and versatile graduate degree around. It can open up many doors of opportunity, providing its holders with cutting-edge knowledge, wealth, and a valuable network of over-achieving colleagues. Gaining admission can be exceedingly competitive, but can prove to be very rewarding over your lifetime. This book can help you accomplish just that.

1
WHY BUSINESS SCHOOL?

- Why do you want to go to business school and why now?
- What do you hope to gain out of business school?
- How will business school help you in your career?

Before you spend the time (and money) to begin this process, you had better know the answers to the above questions. Answering these questions will accomplish three things:

1. Once you know what you want out of business school, it will make your search for the right school much more focused and meaningful.

2. Once your goals are clear, it will help you in crafting your application. Your essays will be much more compelling to the reader, and you can project your goals to your recommenders who will write much more meaningful letters of recommendation.

3. Knowing why you are in business school will help you in taking the right classes and joining the right organizations according to your interests and career goals. The recruiting process starts early, with

companies visiting campuses the very first semester. Being focused on day one of business school will help you in interacting with recruiters and landing that summer position.

Why do you want to go to business school and why now?

What is your reason for applying to business school? Is it because you're an investment banker completing a two-year training program, and an MBA is the next logical step? Do you want to change careers? Is an MBA necessary in order for you to move ahead within your organization? Do you want to launch a start-up while attending business school? There is no right answer to this question; every applicant has his or her reason for applying- and you should be able to state yours intelligently. You also need to be able to answer why you want to go to business school now. Why not next year? Why not five years from now? Why not ten years from now?

Before going off to business school, I worked at Marsh, Inc. for a little under three years. Marsh is a financial firm, and the world leader when it comes to insurance and risk management. I began my career at Marsh in fast-track program, acquiring technical knowledge in risk management, insurance principles, corporate finance and consultative selling, while working on client accounts. Through working on client accounts for two years, I acquired working knowledge of a variety of industries, from manufacturing and real estate to HVAC (heating, ventilation and air conditioning) and retail. Those two years gave me a solid foundation in client service and consulting. Afterwards, I was invited to work on the broking side of our business for a little under a year. There, I negotiated with insurance companies to obtain carrier placements for large commercial accounts. As a broker, I worked on a greater number of client accounts and became familiar with more industries.

Fall 2005 was a great time in my career to begin an MBA program. I just finished learning the broking side of our business and was ready to acquire more high-level skills. After spending a year as a broker, the next step would have been to take my client and broking experience and return to the client management side to start building a client base once again. However, at the time, I had learned all the insurance I wanted to learn, and wanted to return to school to help me transition into corporate finance and, eventually, my own business. It was also a great time to leave before I was buried deep in accounts.

What do you hope to gain out of business school?

Before going into business school, you must know what you want out of it. Are you going to help you find a better job within the same industry? Do you want to graduate with a job in another career? Maybe you hope to work for or run a start-up upon graduation. Every business school offers a different twist to the business school curriculum, different professors and even different opportunities. Knowing what you want out of business school will help you choose the right one for you.

How will business school help you in your career?

The value of an MBA varies among different industries and careers. In some careers, such as management consulting or banking, an MBA from a top school is almost vital for progression. In other fields, like insurance, experience is much more highly regarded than the degree itself. Know how an MBA is valued in your field. An MBA may not be a necessary for success in your career. Or, it may be crucial for moving into management.

2
WHAT ARE BUSINESS SCHOOLS LOOKING FOR?

Before you can craft your application to convince business schools that they absolutely must accept you, you must first know what they want in a prospective student. Through the different parts of your application, your grades, test scores, essays and letters of recommendation, these traits should become evident to the admissions team. Business schools are generally looking for candidates with the characteristics below:

- **Leadership/ management experience from inside and/or outside of the office.** From within the office, have you supervised a group of employees? Have you led project teams? Don't forget about any leadership roles you've had as part of an extracurricular or volunteer activity. Maybe you were in charge of a fundraiser or were a mentor in an after-school program. Those with atypical backgrounds (ie. military or non-profits) usually have an easier time standing out than those from the much more common management consulting or banking backgrounds.

- **Intellectual horsepower.** Earning an MBA is an academically demanding two years and business schools want to be sure that you can handle the load. They'll attempt to predict your future performance partly by looking at your past coursework and GMAT scores. Business schools will typically view those with high GMAT scores and an abundance of analytical coursework in subjects such as statistics, economics and calculus as more favorable candidates. If you were a liberal arts major, you may want to take some analytical courses to show that you have the aptitude for those types of classes.

- **A commitment to others.** Have you been very involved with a charity that means something to you? Are you active in a community or volunteer group? These activities, particularly when done sincerely, can score points in your application.

- **Risk takers.** Business schools want students who will challenge themselves and not take courses for the easy "A." For this reason, some schools discourage recruiters from asking students about their grades. A successful businessperson takes risks, albeit calculated ones. Highlighting some of the risks you've taken in your career, and in certain parts of your life, describing the reward- or loss- and most importantly what you've learned, may help you stand out from others who've simply played it safe most of the time.

- **People great at working with others.** Organizations and business schools alike typically desire someone who works well within a team.

- **Candidates with an overall potential for success.** If you have a positive track record at your job or have been progressing throughout your career you will have an advantage here. Schools will look at your work history for increasing responsibilities-and salaries-over time. If you've gone from job to job with no real upward movement, you must find a way to put a positive spin on it.

3

CHOOSING THE RIGHT PROGRAM

The traditional two-year MBA

Most students choose to pursue the traditional two-year MBA. The first year is typically designed to provide students with a general foundation in business, and usually consists of courses in management, finance, marketing, operations, economics, strategy and technology. At some programs, all students take the exact same courses the first year. The advantage here is that it gives students the opportunity to get to know one another. The disadvantage is the lack of flexibility. During the second year of business school, students pick from a group electives. Some programs require students to pick a concentration, while most programs nowadays allow students to simply pick courses commensurate with their interests. Many will even allow students to cross-register in classes at other graduate programs at the campus.

The one-year MBA

Some schools offer an intensive one-year MBA track. Many European programs are exclusively one-year programs. If you don't like the idea of giving up two years of income, or if you want to go back to school and then return to the same company or industry, a one-year program may be for you. Because of the shorter duration, many companies are more willing to sponsor employees for one-year programs. Additionally, many are more affordable than their two-year counterparts. However, in general, one-year programs tend not to be as comprehensive as two-year programs. And if you are trying to change careers, a one-year program may not give you enough of a foundation to pursue another career. Nevertheless, a one-year program is definitely worth looking into, particularly if you want to return to the workforce quickly. Be sure to weigh out all of the options.

Executive MBA (EMBA)

For employees specifically looking to complement their management experience and move into an executive-level position, an Executive MBA may be appropriate. Designed for more experienced managers, such programs usually require at least six years of management experience. In contrast to the typical MBA student who has four years of post-undergraduate work experience, many EMBA students have ten or even fifteen years of work experience. If you are an experienced manager, and senior management is the next step for you, you may want to look into an EMBA program.

One-year specialized Masters (MS)

Many schools also offer a specialized Master's degree in areas such as general management, finance, technology, supply chain management or manufacturing. A traditional MBA is typically designed to groom general managers. However, an MS may be appropriate for you if your needs are more specialized. MIT offers a Master of Engineering in Logistics (MLOG) program for those seeking careers in logistics and supply chain management. The Haas School of Business at Berkeley offers students seeking comprehensive technical knowledge in the financial markets the option of pursuing a Master's in Financial Engineering.

Full-time or part-time?

Full-time

Attending school full-time is a big commitment. Many of the top schools only offer full-time programs. Due to the demanding nature of the program, employment during the school year is typically not permitted. If you are considering a full-time program, you should factor into your budget the opportunity cost of forgone income. However, attending a full-time program with other full-time students often allows for better networking opportunities and a more communal feel to the program. If you're looking to change careers, it will probably be much easier to do so in a full-time program.

If you're thinking of enrolling in a full-time program, consider the following:

- **Factor in the opportunity cost of no full-time income for two years.** Some part-time programs can be done in two years, without having to give up your current income.

- **Find out if your company will sponsor you for full-time enrollment.** Some will, provided you agree to a commitment afterwards, ranging anywhere from one to five years. A one-year commitment may not sound like much, but if you're trying to change careers, it may hamper your networking opportunities.

Part-time

A part-time program may be more appropriate if you are on a career track at your company and want an MBA to help you advance. Many companies pay for promising employees to pursue MBA's part-time. A part-time program will enable you to work full-time and advance in your career *while* you earn your MBA. And even if it has to come out of your own pocket, you don't have to give up your full-time salary in the process. However, holding down a full-time job and going to school will involve some very long days. Your class schedule may be from 6pm until about 9 or 10pm, two or three times a week. And so, after a grueling day at the office, provided you're able to leave on time, be ready to drive to class in rush hour traffic for the next three or four years. If you have a demanding job, it may be hard to focus on your studies. You may find yourself late to class regularly or unable to study as often as you'd like.

If you're thinking of enrolling in a part-time program, consider the following:

- **Logistics.** Consider your commute time and distance from the office to school, and then back home.

- **Determine whether your schedule can handle the demands of going to school part-time.** Would the nature of your job allow for school in the evenings? Does your job involve a lot of traveling? You may want to look into a part-time program that accommodates professionals such as yourself. With the Internet, you may be able to complete school assignments while away on business.

- **Decide if you are a good fit for a part-time program.** Are you the type of person who wants to really network and take advantage of many of the things business school has to offer? Do you want to network and participate in clubs and associations? Do you want to get to know your fellow students and professors? This may prove to be a difficult feat if you're working sixty to seventy hours per week while attending school.

Which school?

There are hundreds of graduate business programs in the United States alone. So how do you decide which one to go to? What makes one better than the other? I am always reluctant to use the word "better" when referring to business schools. Instead, find a school that is better for *you*. Find one that is a great match for what you want out of a business program and that better suits your personal and professional needs. This is why it is so important to establish what it is you want out of business school from the beginning. In deciding which schools to apply to, many potential applicants rely too heavily on published rankings. There are two major flaws in this approach:

1. **Just because one program is ranked higher than another does not mean that the program is better for *you*.** Many other factors should be considered as well, including the size, cost, location and quality of life, among others.

2. **There are a number of different rankings out there, all with different criteria for evaluating business schools.** For example, at the time of this writing, Stanford is ranked #2 on US News, but #30 in the Wall Street Journal guide.

While it is important to know what the rankings are, they alone should not dictate the schools to which you apply. Instead, rankings should be used solely as guides. There are many other factors which should be considered when deciding where to earn your MBA, including:

- Cost
- Size
- Academic programs
- Employment statistics
- Location of school

Cost

Business school can be an expensive education. Here's a sample student budget for business school:

February 2004 2004-2005 MBA Student Budgets for Class of 2006			
	Single	Married	Married and One Child
Tuition	$35,600	$35,600	$35,600
Health Services Fee	1,264	2,854	4,116
Blue Cross/ Blue Shield	1,448	3,264	4,720
Program Support Fee	3,500	3,500	3,500
Room & Utilities (9 months)	11,270	13,670	17,820
Board, Personal, Other	11,018	14,012	18,344
TOTAL	$64,100	$72,900	$84,100

Although cost should be a factor, it should not be an overwhelming one. Many top programs guarantee access to financing to cover the entire student budget. A large number of students receive some form of financial aid. The cost of a program should not prohibit you from going to your dream school. Additionally, you want to look at a school's return on investment (ROI). A private school may cost more than some other programs in terms of tuition, but may pay off far more over your lifetime in the form of a higher salary, stronger network or other intangible benefits. However, you may want to compare the costs of private and public school programs. Examine your financial situation and determine whether or not your budget allows for such an investment.

Size

Do you want to attend a large or small program? Each has its advantages, so it's important to determine the better fit for you. Here are a few of the bigger programs:

Program	Enrollment
Columbia	1,762
Harvard	1,808
Kellogg	2,720
Michigan	1,939
Wharton	1,950

Here are a few of the smaller programs:

Program	Enrollment
Cornell	659
Emory	638
MIT	744
Tuck	463
Yale	481

Big vs. small schools

Factor	Bigger School	Smaller School
Resources (books, technology, facilities, etc.)	Typically more	Typically less
Class size	Larger; typically less opportunities to speak.	Smaller; more opportunities to shine in the classroom.
Environment	Less personal; sometimes more of a factory-like approach	Typically closer-knit

Big vs. small schools (cont.)

Factor	Bigger School	Smaller School
Your presence	More likely to get lost in the shuffle	More likely to stand out
Number of recruiters	Typically more	Typically less
Academic programs	Typically wider selection of classes and majors	Typically narrower selection of classes and majors
Alumni Network	Larger alumni network	Smaller, but sometimes more closely knit of an alumni network

Employment Statistics

Business school is a big investment. When it's all over, it would be great to have a job that meets your career interests. For the most part, the major firms recruit at all of the top-ten business schools. However, it's important to look at employment statistics at the program you are interested in. Employment statistics are usually available on the school's website.

When taking a look at employment statistics, consider the following:

- **Know which companies recruit there.** If you want to work for a big management consulting firm like McKinsey or BoozAllen upon graduation, your odds of employment are far better if the schools actively recruit at your business school.

- **Look where students tend to work after graduation.** If you plan on living on the east coast after earning your MBA, a strong alumni presence there may work to your advantage. Additionally, if the majority of graduates tend to work in proximity to the school, the school may not have a strong presence across other parts of the country.

- **Pay attention to starting salaries by job function.** It is important to use this as a guide and not as an unrealistic benchmark. First of all, not all students report their income. Second of all, don't view the listed average starting salary as guaranteed. Compensation packages are commensurate with skills and experience, along with education.

How to research schools

An important part of the admissions process is the research of several programs in order to find the one that suits you. Your research should incorporate the following:

- **Visit the school website.** Learn about its culture, academic programs, methods of instruction, admissions and financial aid requirements, etc.

- **Attend information sessions in your area.** Many
  schools will advertise information sessions in your
  hometown on their websites. Register on their email lists
  to receive periodic updates.

- **Visit the campus.** I am amazed at how many applicants
  do not even visit their first-choice program before
  applying. Make an attempt to visit your top choices.
  Visiting the campus will give you a better feel for the
  environment. Additionally, it will give you the
  opportunity to sit in on classes and talk to students,
  alumni and faculty. Getting some face time may help tip
  the scale in your favor during the admissions process.
  Some programs have structured weekend programs for
  prospective students. I visited my top choices- Michigan,
  Dartmouth, Harvard and Stanford. Before deciding to
  attend Michigan, I attended *Go Blue! Rendezvous*, a
  three-day event on-campus for admitted students. After
  attending this event, I knew that Michigan was the right
  fit for me. A friend of mine was a first-year student at
  HBS, and so, I visited the campus and sat in on one of
  his classes. At Stanford, I attended an all day event for
  prospective students. There, I spoke to students, alumni,
  and faculty. It also gave me the opportunity to listen to
  student panels and ask questions about the program. At
  Dartmouth, I participated in a weekend program for
  minority students. I stayed in the dorm of a first-year
  student, and met many other current students and alumni.
  It was great to participate in these programs and meet
  other prospective students- some of whom I still keep in

touch with. To make a long story short- visit some campuses!

- **Read outside texts on different programs.** Sometimes an outside text can provide you with an unbiased perspective about a program. *The WSJ Guide to the Top Business Schools* ranks each school according to recruiter ratings. It also includes positive and negative comments commonly made by recruiters about each program.

Research scholarship opportunities

Believe it or not, scholarships are available for business school. Be sure to utilize the Internet in your search for business school funds. Below are some sites that you may find helpful. I applied to business school through the Consortium for Graduate Study in Management, which enabled me to attend Michigan with a full ride.

- Consortium for Graduate Study in Management, www.cgsm.org
- Diversity Pipeline Alliance, www.diversitypipeline.com
- Leadership Education and Development Program in Business (LEAD), www.leadnational.org
- Management Leadership for Tomorrow, www.ml4t.org
- National Black M.B.A. Association, www.nbmbaa.org
- National Society of Hispanic M.B.A.'s, www.nshmba.org
- Robert Toigo Foundation, www.rtf.org

4

TAKING THE GMAT

To many applicants, the GMAT is the scariest part of the admissions process. It is a three-hour exam, consisting of:

- Two thirty minute essays
- A 75 minute math section
- A 75 minute verbal section

The exam is not to be taken lightly. It is important to take the exam seriously and to dismiss the notion that you can simply show up and "wing it." Although a high score does not guarantee admission to a top program, a low score can keep you out of one. It is far better, and less expensive, to allot the necessary study time to do well on your first try than to take it multiple times. Also, know how each school you are interested in will treat multiple scores. Your last five results will appear in your score report, and will be viewed by schools. Some will count only the highest, while others may simply take an average.

The GMAT is used as a standard measure of academic ability and can tell admissions personnel a lot about an applicant. An applicant with an average score who makes no attempt to improve it may be viewed as complacent with mediocrity. And an applicant who aces it the first time may be viewed as someone with the intellectual ability necessary to survive business school. Pay attention to the average GMAT scores of the schools you are interested in. While the average score for all test-takers is about a 520, the average GMAT score for entering students at the top programs is around 700.

Should I self-study or take a course?

Your answer to this question could mean the difference between success and failure on this exam. In answering it, you must examine yourself and acknowledge how you learn best. If you can learn independently, you may do just fine self-studying for the exam. However, if you prefer concepts to be taught to you, or if you have been out of school for an extended period of time, classroom instruction may be for you.

When I began to study for the GMAT, I had been out of college for just two years. Additionally, I had self-studied for six industry exams during my two years at Marsh. That said, I was comfortable with the idea of self-studying for another exam. I started with the Princeton Review book, which comes with four full-length computer adaptive (CAT) exams- similar to the actual exam. This book had great explanations of the sections and of the different types of problems on the GMAT. After reviewing the sections over the next two weeks, I took a practice exam and scored a 590. I continued to perform practice problems in the book and take practice CAT exams every week. My scores on the remainder of the exams were in the 610 to 640 range. The use of flashcards helped me study in college, and so, I made GMAT flashcards. I took these flashcards with me to work and studied them whenever I got the chance, whether on the train or during a lunch break. During my three months of studying for the exam, I made over a hundred of them. I made the following types of flashcards:

- **I made flashcards of difficult types of problems.** On one side of the card was the question, and on the other side was the solution. This helped me memorize an approach to the problems I had difficulty with.

- **I made flashcards of concepts and strategies.** Time during the exam will zoom by, and you may not have time to stop and remember a grammar rule, or an approach to a Critical Reasoning question involving cause and effect. I turned proven approaches and strategies into flashcards to help internalize them.

While flipping through different GMAT prep books at the bookstore, I noticed that each one was quite different. Some were better at explaining different sections and others had better strategies and approaches for certain sections. Additionally, each had different practice problems and different practice CAT exams. Hence, I decided that my studying would be more effective if I used different prep books that complemented one another. After Princeton Review, I used the Kaplan 800 book, which claims to focus solely on the difficult problems. Then, I used the ARCO book, which had great tutorials for each section. Finally, I bought the regular Kaplan prep book, which comes with four very difficult CAT exams. If you prepare with Kaplan's exams, be aware that they are very difficult; many argue that they are even more difficult than the actual GMAT. Taking their exams trained me to work under a clock with the most difficult problems.

While reviewing book after book, I continued to make my flashcards and take practice CAT exams. I took at least one practice CAT exam every week. By the test date, I had taken about fifteen full-length practice CAT exams. The importance of taking practice exams cannot be stressed enough. Doing it helps develop your rhythm and pacing-crucial if you want to get a great score. I took the actual GMAT once and scored a 730. I took it in October, the year before I wanted to start school, to give me enough time just in case I needed to retake it.

Below is what my study schedule looked like. I have included it here to show you how much studying I had to do to perform well on this exam. And even after all of this studying, the exam was still difficult. I am not telling you to follow this exact schedule, but it should give you an idea of the hard work involved in studying for the GMAT.

Kaine's GMAT Study Schedule	
Week	**Activity**
1	Bought Princeton Review book. Read math section.
2	Read Verbal section. Took practice CAT exam 1 (590).
3	Did practice problems and made flashcards. Took practice CAT exam 2 (640).
4	Did practice problems and made flashcards. Took practice CAT exam 3 (640).
5	Did practice problems and made flashcards. Took practice CAT exam 4 (610).
6	Did practice problems and made flashcards. Retook a Princeton practice CAT exam (640).
7	Bought Kaplan GMAT 800 book. Studied the Verbal section. Made flashcards. Registered for the actual GMAT. Took practice CAT exam 6 by Cambridge (640).
8	Studied the Math section of the GMAT 800 book and made more flashcards; took practice CAT exams 7 & 8 by Cambridge (610 & 640).
9	Read the ARCO book; Made more flashcards; took practice CAT exam 9 by Cambridge (660).
10	Read the Kaplan GMAT guide (with the four CAT exams). Took Kaplan CAT exam 10 and scored a 620.

Kaine's GMAT Study Schedule (cont.)	
Week	**Activity**
11	Continued to work through Kaplan's practice problems. Took more Cambridge practice exams 11 & 12 and scored a 640 and 680.
12	Took another Cambridge CAT exam 13 and scored a 650. Took the Powerprep (ETS) CAT exams 14 & 15 and scored a 710 and 730 respectively. Took the actual GMAT on Saturday and scored a 730. (quantitative-46; verbal- 45) Celebrated after a job well done!

GMAT Myths

- **You're a "shoe-in" if you score above a 700.** This is not necessarily true. The exam is an important factor in the admissions process, but only one factor. Business schools evaluate applications as a whole when making decisions. For the same reason, a GMAT score below the school's mean does not necessarily disqualify you either.

- **You need an expensive course to score well on the exam.** Absolutely false. If you can pick up things on your own, you can learn the GMAT with time and dedication. A course is fine, if you learn better with an instructor. However, a course is not the easy way to success on the GMAT. To maximize success, classroom instruction must be complemented with many hours of practice on your own. An expensive course does not guarantee a high score. I have friends who have achieved just average scores after enrolling in courses that cost almost as much as my first car.

- **You can't study for the GMAT; either you know it or you don't.** Not true. The concepts on the GMAT can be learned and practiced. When I first began taking practice exams, I was averaging in the low 600's. Right before the exam, I was averaging in the low 700's. When it comes to the GMAT, practice definitely makes perfect.

- **Since I'm good at math, I shouldn't have to study for the GMAT.** Think again. GMAT math is not everyday math. If you do consider yourself to be a "math-whiz," at least review the types of math questions asked on the GMAT, and do NOT walk into the test cold.

General tips for the GMAT

- **If you choose to self-study for the GMAT, use more than one guide.** Not all GMAT guides are created equally. Different prep books have different strengths. Use multiple guides that complement each other's weaknesses. I recommend using at least two or three if you're aiming for a great score.

- **If you do choose to take a course, do your homework.** Talk to current and past students. Find out the company's retake policy. Some will let you continue to take additional classes at no additional charge if you bomb the exam. Be realistic about your expectations. An expensive course is not necessarily the easy way to a high score. It will still require long and grueling hours on your part.

- **Take multiple full-length practice CAT exams.** I cannot stress this enough. You need to train yourself to stare at a computer screen for three hours without becoming mentally exhausted. Additionally, you'll get better at pacing yourself through the exam. You'll know which types of problems you'll need more time on, and which ones you can breeze through. I took about fifteen practice CAT exams before the actual GMAT. Practice makes perfect.

- **Perform practice problems from every section during each of your study sessions.** After you've spent a couple weeks learning all the sections, I don't recommend focusing a week on one section, and then another week on another section. For example, do fifteen practice problems from each section every study session. This will train your mind to switch gears from one type of problem to another- a skill you'll need the day of the exam.

- **When taking practice exams, simulate testing conditions as much as possible.** Don't get up during the test to grab some food or to turn the radio on. However, do get up during the five-minute breaks to stretch and to use the restroom. Additionally, take your practice tests at the same date and time as your scheduled GMAT exam. For example, if you are registered for Saturday at 8A.M., be sure to take a practice exam every Saturday at 8 A.M. This will get your mind used to thinking at that time of day.

- **Get a good night's sleep the night before.** Your mind will be more alert when you do. Eat a small breakfast before the exam, and most of all- relax!

5
WORK EXPERIENCE

How important is work experience?

The classroom environment in business school is entirely different from that of undergrad. In an undergraduate-level lecture, the professor is responsible for teaching the material. The students' role is to absorb that material, and may ask questions or participate in the classroom with the aim of reinforcing the material presented by the professor. In a business school classroom, the students have a much more active role in the educational process. The professor is more of a facilitator of discussion than a teacher. The professor mostly guides the classroom discussion and challenges students to think and solve problems.

The students do much of the teaching in a business school classroom. A business school classroom is comprised of students from a variety of backgrounds- from different countries, professions and industries, and with different values and upbringings. In the classroom, students are expected to bring knowledge and experience to the table that their fellow classmates can learn from. No wonder most top schools want at least two years of professional experience (average is about four years). In fact, it is nearly impossible to get into a top-ten business school without any post-undergraduate work experience.

Acquiring some real-world experience before returning to school helps you as well. Your developmental needs will become more apparent after some years in the working world. For example, you may have an interest in finance, but after working in your chosen profession, you may discover that you really need more specialized training in marketing. Hence, some work experience will make your two years in business school much more meaningful. You will get much more out of it.

How much work experience should you have?

There is no universal answer to this question. Some professionals return to business school after just two years, some after ten years. Business schools are more concerned with the quality of your experience rather than the quantity. They want to see that your work experience has enabled you to grow.

Finding your answer will involve some analysis of where you are in your career and where you want to go. Are you at the point where you can go as far as you can go with a Bachelor's? I felt ready to return to school after working for a little under three years. That gave me enough time to acquire a solid technical foundation in the insurance industry. Afterwards, I was ready to acquire more finance, strategy and entrepreneurship skills.

Think long and hard about how an MBA in combination with your work experience will promote your career and meet your long-term objectives- and be ready to explain it. You'll be expected to describe this in your application essays and during your interviews. If you can't explain this intelligently, you may want to reevaluate your reasons for getting an MBA.

6
LETTERS OF RECOMMENDATION

Most business school applications will require at least one letter of recommendation. Many of the top programs want three. Below are typical requirements at top programs:

- At least two letters of recommendation should be from a professional context.
- At least one recommendation should be from a direct supervisor (this does not apply to college seniors).
- The third recommendation can be written by a professional, extracurricular, or academic reference.

When I put together my list of recommenders, I chose the following people:

- **A senior colleague at my current job.** He was the perfect person to validate my on-the-job responsibilities and accomplishments. He had a hand in training me when I first started with the firm, and I have worked with him on numerous accounts and projects since then.

- **A past employer.** I maintained a great relationship with the CEO of a small firm where I worked for a year during college. She could speak to the teams and projects I led during my employment there.

- **The pastor of my church.** I had been very active in my church for the past nine years. During that period of time, I managed and coordinated play productions, mentored teenagers and taught workshops on personal finance. He could attest to some of my activities outside of the office.

This was a good mix of people who could confirm the different activities and accomplishments alluded to in my application.

How important are letters of recommendations?

A good letter of recommendation will help backup the professional experience presented in the rest of your application, particularly, your resume and your essays. Therefore, choose your recommenders wisely. Each of your recommendations should be consistent with the information provided in the rest of your application. Any of the following could signal a red flag to an admissions committee:

- **What you say you did at a job doesn't match up with what one of your recommenders says you actually did there.** For example, you say in your resume and in your essays that you supervised five employees at XYZ Corp., and your recommender, a manager at XYZ Corp., says that you didn't supervise any.

- **One of your recommenders has some reservations about recommending you to business school.** If a person *you* pick to speak on your behalf cannot recommend you with confidence, what message does that send?

- **Your recommendations appear sloppy, without much time or effort taken to complete them.** Writing a recommendation can be a very time consuming endeavor. Make sure your recommenders care about you enough to take the time and care this process requires.

- **The writing style of your recommendations has a striking resemblance to that of your essays.** Be cautious about even drafting a recommendation letter for your contact to edit and submit. Many top schools highly discourage this, and claim to be able to spot a self-written recommendation.

So just how important are recommendations? Well-written recommendations consistent with the overall theme of a strong application can reaffirm an applicant in the eyes of an admissions committee. Usually, however, they will not turn the tides for an applicant with weak grades or GMAT scores.

Here are some general tips for obtaining effective letters of recommendations:

- **Ask early.** I recommend asking at least a month before the deadline. Give them enough time to write something meaningful that will help your cause.

- **Choose your writers wisely.** Pick people who know you well and can cite specific examples that will strengthen your application. This is more important than choosing famous recommenders or those with important sounding titles. If the person seems apprehensive about writing it, choose someone else.

- **Meet with your writers beforehand to discuss your goals.** Make each one aware of your career goals and what you want out of business school. Give them a copy of your resume and a summary of the points you want them to touch on in their recommendations.

- **Follow up with each writer and make sure they submit it before the deadline.** To be on the safe side, you may even want to impose a deadline a week before the actual deadline.

7

EXTRACURRICULAR ACTIVITIES

Business schools are also interested in how you spend your time outside of the office. If you are an active member of any clubs or organizations, this could work to your advantage. Use caution in mentioning activities that indicate ideological or religious views.

Highlight activities that:

- Helped you grow professionally and/or personally
- Show your commitment to helping others.
- Help you emphasize positive traits, like leadership or teamwork.

Here's a list of some of the extracurricular activities I participated in before I attended business school:

- **Beta Gamma Sigma, Member, Los Angeles, CA Chapter, 2002 to 2005**
  Beta Gamma Sigma is the honor society serving business programs accredited by AACSB International - The Association to Advance Collegiate Schools of

Business. Membership in Beta Gamma Sigma is the highest recognition a business student anywhere in the world can receive in a business program accredited by AACSB International.

- **Toastmasters Organization, Member, Los Angeles, CA, 2002 to 2005**
  Toastmaster's is the world's leading communication and leadership development organization. It provides an environment where its members can hone their public speaking skills, both planned and impromptu.

- **Lifeline International Ministries, Play writer and director, 1995 to 2004**
  Here I lead and managed teenagers in the writing, casting and production of plays for Christmas and Easter services.

- **Inroads Expo Participant, Los Angeles, CA, 2004**
  The purpose of the event was to educate university students about Marsh, and about career opportunities within the firm and the industry. As a part of the event, I was assigned to a group of students and coached them on their interview skills and also provided feedback on their resumes.

- **City of Hope Walk- 5K Participant, Duarte, CA, 2003**
  To support breast cancer research, treatment and education at the City of Hope National Medical Center and Beckman Research Institute.

8
INTERVIEWS

The interview is an opportunity for schools to put a name to a face, and to get to know you on a more personal level. At the top business schools, an interview is required for admission and is by invitation only. So if you don't receive an invitation to interview, you won't be offered admission either.

Chances are, if you're invited to interview at a school, you are looked upon as a strong candidate for admission. However, schools usually admit less than half of the students who are interviewed. And so, if you're lucky enough to be invited to interview at a top program, be aware that the journey is not yet over.

Here are some general tips for business school interviews and, in some cases, interviews in general:

- **Stay calm and poised no matter what question you are asked.** Some interviewers will ask off-the-wall questions just to observe your reaction.

- **Unless instructed otherwise, dress in business professional attire.** This means wear a professional looking suit (and tie if you're a male).

- **Send the interviewer a thank you note after the interview.**

- **Get to the interview about ten minutes before schedule.** You never want to be late- or too early for that matter. About ten minutes early is appropriate.

- **Ask two or three challenging questions at the end of the interview.** An interview is also an opportunity for you to learn more about the program. Asking questions shows your interest.

Common interview questions

- Why do you want to attend this program?
- What will you bring to this school that is unique?
- How will an MBA enhance your career and long-term goals?
- What do you want out of business school?
- Tell me about a leadership role you had.
- Tell me about a failure and what you learned from it.
- What is your most important accomplishment?
- Tell me about an ethical dilemma and how you dealt with it.
- At what moment in your career did you realize that an MBA might be helpful or even necessary?

9

ADMISSIONS ESSAYS

Your grades are a part of the past, you've taken the GMAT, your writers are working on their letters of recommendation and your work history is just that- history. When it comes down to it, writing your admissions essays is the one task you have *complete* control over. Nevertheless, many applicants simply view the essays as yet another administrative part of the application that can be rushed through. Don't make that mistake. While a stellar essay alone won't lock in admission for an otherwise sub par candidate, poorly written essays can certainly jeopardize admission for an otherwise qualified one.

So what should you write about in your essays? Well, it goes back to our discussion of the types of people business schools want. As we discussed, business schools generally favor applicants with the following characteristics:

- Leadership/ management experience from inside and/or outside of the office
- Intellectual horsepower
- A commitment to others
- People great at working with others
- Candidates with an overall potential for success

A solid application will show, not tell, these qualities. Don't write about how hard working you are, how great you are with people, or about how great you are at leading a team. Instead, show these qualities through the examples you write about. Let the admissions committee draw positive conclusions about you based on what they read in your essays.

Writing your business school essays will promise to be a gut-wrenching, soul-searching experience. Don't underestimate the importance of it. Take your time and do it right.

Here are some general tips on writing admissions essays:

- **Have someone else read them.** Get someone who knows you well to review and discuss them with you. Sometimes an outside reader will be able to provide some useful insight.

- **Adhere to the word limits.** If the word limit on an essay is 600 words, don't write 1,000. You may be OK if you write 610 or even 650. However, you're better off staying within the limits specified.

- **Proofread for typographical or grammatical errors.** Such errors can make your essays seem unpolished. Look out for mistakes your computer's spell-check might miss, like "too" instead of "to."

- **Revise, revise, and revise!** Chances are, you won't write a winning essay on a first, second or third draft; so don't be afraid to put your nose to the grindstone. Constantly revising your essays will help you think of more effective ways to state your case. Additionally, it will help you catch typographical and grammatical errors.

Below are approaches and sample responses to common essay questions. You'll notice that while I cut and pasted where I could, I also tailored each essay to each program. You never want to write generic essays that will be used for more than one application. You always want to customize your responses to the program you're applying to. "Cut and paste" is a great tool but use it with caution. There's nothing worse than saying you really want to go to Wharton Business School in your Harvard essay.

Sample approaches to common essay topics

Describe a significant change you brought about in an organization and its impact on your development as a leader.

With a question like this, the actual change you brought about is usually less important than its impact on your professional development. Many applicants spend a lot of time explaining the details of the project they worked on, and forget to highlight how they grew as a result of the situation. The following is one possible outline for this type of question:

- **Introduce the problem or issue.** Maybe you noticed an inefficient process within your firm.

- **Discuss your role in the solution and the changes you spearheaded.** It is important to emphasize your specific role if you worked within part of a team.

- **Describe how working on the project made you a more effective leader as a result.** Did you get better at dealing with difficult employees or clients?

What are three accomplishments you are proud of?

This is always a tricky question. Business schools want to know what is important to you. My advice is for you to choose three accomplishments you are truly proud of- not what you think business schools might want to hear. Be cautious about discussing something already mentioned in another part of your application, like grades or tests scores. If you do, make sure to emphasize the reason these things are so important to you, and not the accomplishment itself.

Provide a candid assessment of your strengths and weaknesses.

Here's another golden question. Instead of firing off a list of adjectives, you may want to include situations that show your strengths. For example, instead of saying that your strengths are that you are good with people and a great team player, you may want to try bringing up a past situation that shows you have these traits. In answering this question, brainstorm what you think your strengths are, and then think of a way to show them through a story.

The same strategy may be employed when talking about your weaknesses. Then you may want to explain what you do to overcome those weaknesses. Put a positive spin on the negative whenever possible.

How do you define success?

Again, business schools want to know what you value. Is money what drives you? Or does helping others fulfill you? Be honest. A good response to this question will illustrate a definition of success by using concrete examples.

What are your career aspirations and how can an MBA help you reach them? Why now?

Here, it is important to describe how you think your past experience combined with an MBA will help you achieve your long-term goals. What role does the MBA have in your professional development? Could you accomplish the same goals without an MBA? Why do you want an MBA from this school?

What do you wish the MBA Admissions Board had asked you?

Here's an opportunity to discuss something to advance your cause that may not have been addressed in other parts of your application. Use it wisely.

What matters most to you, and why?

Here, describing the "why" is perhaps far more important than talking about the "what." How has your professional development, management style, personal life, etc. been influenced?

What are your short-term and long-term career aspirations? How will an MBA education further your development? Why does the academic experience offered at this school appeal to you?

Answering this question will involve the following:

- An in-depth analysis of what you want out of business school in general
- A thorough research of this program
- Connecting the dots between your work experience, what you're looking to get out of this program and what you plan to do after receiving your MBA.

Business schools don't expect you to have your entire life figured out. However, they typically would like to see that you've thought of a post-MBA plan and that you've done enough homework on their program to discuss intelligently how it fits into your plan.

Sample responses to common essay topics

Describe a significant change you brought about in an organization and its impact on your development as a leader.

During my first year at Marsh, I recognized a need within the company. Although the company had a structured training program in place for Graduates, (the participants in an intensive one-year program) no formalized orientation program existed for new employees. As a result, most new employees were ignorant of the roles of other sister companies and departments, technical resources within the organization, job functions of other colleagues and the criteria for promotion within the organization.

After interviewing members of our senior management to find out the information they thought was important for new hires to know, I compiled the results of my research and presented a solution. I proposed to senior management that we do two things. First, that we put together a written guide containing information important to new employees. Second, that we conduct mini-seminars, perhaps during lunchtime, where department managers educate new employees about the roles and functions of their departments.

Management liked the idea and put me in charge of the project. The guide would give an overview of the organization and the different departments, licensing and designation requirements, client team roles and technological resources. Because of the size of the task, I delegated the copying and assembling to other colleagues. Once the fifty-five-page book was completed, our Human Resources department gave it to new employees and used it as a template for the western region of the firm.

Along with the written guide, I initiated informational workshops for newer employees. During each workshop, a department manager talked about the roles and functions of his department and opened up a question and answer session. The workshops were successful at educating newer employees about other areas of the company.

This was one of the first projects at Marsh that I managed from start to finish. I saw a need within the organization, and then proposed and implemented the solution. The success of this project taught me that although I was new to the company, I could take a leadership role in a project and make a valuable contribution. When I become a manager, I will expect the same initiative from all employees, old and new.

Provide a candid assessment of your strengths and weaknesses.

A consciousness of my strengths and weaknesses has been invaluable to my professional development. The learning curve in our industry is very high and it can take years to achieve the level of technical proficiency necessary to serve clients effectively. However, I not only have the intellectual ability to absorb technical information quickly, but also the patience and work ethic necessary in order to do so. While it takes many associates at least five years before they can handle accounts independently, I began to do so after only one year.

Initially, an obstacle was my youth. Many of my clients are older and much more seasoned in the corporate world. But my ability to build rapport, listen to and internalize their needs, and communicate ideas to them helped me gain their trust and respect.

My success at Marsh can be partly attributed to my commitment to developing technical and professional skills. In June 2004, I successfully self-studied for and earned an Associate in Risk Management (ARM), a professional designation requiring the completion of six textbooks and the passing of three state exams. In addition, I have passed two exams towards an Associate in Insurance Services (AIS) and plan on earning the designation early next year. In August 2002, I joined the Toastmaster's Organization to develop better public speaking skills. As a member of the organization, I gave planned and impromptu speeches and participated in impromptu debates. Toastmaster's is a great environment to improve because every speaker receives oral and written feedback.

Sometimes I still struggle with juggling an insane amount of projects. As a client manager, clients, management and colleagues pull you in many different directions simultaneously. At times, it is difficult to stay on top of the numerous deadlines without letting one of them slip. However, I stay on top of assignments by making sure that I am extremely organized. Making schedules and keeping a written record of all projects and due dates has help me stay on track and not fall behind.

How do you define success?

Success is using failure and life's setbacks as opportunities to learn, grow and become a stronger person as a result. There was a time when I feared failure. However, this was not a practical approach to life because a fear of failure will discourage me from taking risks that could potentially lead to success. Some believe that you can never fail if you never make an attempt to succeed. However, this is the biggest failure of all. Life is similar to a game of basketball. You can only score if you shoot the ball. Sometimes you will miss, but other times you will not. Of course you can go through the game without missing if you avoid attempting a single shot. However, at the end of the game you have scored nothing. Success is not about avoiding risk to avoid failure, but about taking calculated risks and using failure to learn and increase your odds of success.

A truly successful person has used those experiences to help others achieve success as well. This is a motto I live by, and perhaps the primary reason why I mentor others. I believe that if I had a close mentor before and during college, my college experience would have been much more focused. I had to learn many things on my own. However, I learned immensely from my experiences, and use them to mentor and advise current students or others planning to attend college.

As someone who is first-generation corporate world, I learned a lot through research and trail and error. Much of my knowledge, from how to research companies, interview and network, to the nuances of corporate culture, I acquired through experience and by studying and asking questions. I now use this knowledge to advise college seniors and recent college grads on topics such as resume writing, interview skills and corporate do's and don'ts. With an MBA, I will have even more to offer others in the way of knowledge, experience and contacts. The more I learn and achieve, the more I have to give. That is success.

What are your career aspirations and how can an MBA help you reach them? Why now?

The two major sides of our business are the client side and the broking side. I began my career at Marsh in fast-track program, acquiring technical knowledge in risk management, insurance principles, corporate finance and consultative selling, while working on client accounts. Through working on client accounts for two years, I acquired working knowledge of a variety of industries, from manufacturing and real estate to HVAC (heating, ventilation and air conditioning) and retail. With a solid foundation in client service and consulting, I fulfilled the role of a "trusted business advisor." Prior to starting graduate school, I will also have a year's experience on the broking side of our business, working and negotiating with insurance companies to obtain carrier placements for large commercial accounts. As a broker, I work on a greater number of client accounts and have become familiar with more industries.

Fall 2005 is a great time in my career to begin an MBA program. I will just have finished learning the broking side of our business and will be ready to acquire more skills. My goal is not to study to become a finance, marketing or technology specialist, but to become a well-rounded leader and business advisor with an excellent foundation in many areas. This is why [Name] Business School is a good fit for me. [School]'s general management curriculum gives its students the freedom to take advantage of a variety of courses without having to specialize in any given discipline. This will enable me to take courses commensurate with my interests and long-term career goals. I am particularly interested in the areas of finance, strategy and entrepreneurship, and plan to participate in field-based learning to apply the skills acquired in the classroom.

An MBA in combination with my professional background will prepare me to become a more effective consultant, entrepreneur and business leader. I plan to take that knowledge and experience and work with not only start-up and growing companies but with growing economies as well. Although there are many opportunities within the United States, there are even more opportunities overseas for trained business leaders. After visiting [School] and talking to students, I was excited to learn that many students share the same interest of starting businesses overseas. A business school is in fact an "incubator of ideas" and the entrepreneurial drive in the students at [School] is truly inspiring. I view other students not only as potential friends, but also as potential business partners and contacts.

What will you bring to [School] that is unique?

When I visited [School] in November, I toured the campus, spoke to first and second-year students, and sat in on a friend's Technology and Operations Management class taught by Professor [Name]. It was an incredible experience to witness the famous [School] case study in action. The diversity of students impressed me the most.

Because students were from different parts of the world, and from different professional backgrounds, it was fascinating to listen to the many perspectives on the case.

I also noticed that no students I met were from my industry. Aside from my ethnicity, I can bring another element of diversity to the classroom. As a professional trained to analyze and manage risk for a wide array of clients, I will bring another perspective to the dynamic case environment. Because of my uncommon background, I will have a lot to offer to my classmates. Many business undergraduates, who typically lust after the management consulting and investment banking positions, often overlook the insurance industry. However, because risk is inherent in every business decision, it is important for leaders in an organization to understand how to identify, quantify and manage risk. Knowledge of global insurance markets is necessary for risks that must be transferred to a third party- a factor especially important for uncommon exposures. This is my background and is something unique that my classmates can learn from me.

Another unique quality that I can bring to [School] is that I have learned leadership skills from inside and outside of the office. Within the office, I have managed clients, projects and teams with great success. I have maintained ongoing relationships with numerous clients, advised them on their business decisions and have managed colleagues to accomplish the surrounding tasks. Outside of the office, I have led and managed over ten play productions, put together financial workshops to help people manage their personal finances and helped some of my peers become better public speakers through the Toastmaster's Organization. Leadership does not begin and end at the workplace, but should encompass every aspect of life.

What matters most to you, and why?

Three things matter most to me. First, a personal commitment to a lifelong development of professional and personal talents. Second, the wisdom to view mistakes and other life experiences as learning opportunities. And third, the desire and ability to use those talents and life experiences to help others.

In the search for a career after college, I wanted to work in an environment where I could develop technical, professional and communication skills. After extensive research, Marsh's Graduate Training Program seemed like the right fit. It is a highly selective, rigorous program designed to accelerate its colleagues' integration into Marsh and make them productive more quickly by supplementing skills learned on the job with formal training in insurance, risk management, accounting, financial analysis and professional skills. It was a great opportunity, and so, I applied to the program. After passing a series of interviews and a one-hour case, I was accepted into the one-year program.

Since the program, I have continued to take steps to develop my technical and professional skills. In June 2004, I successfully self-studied for and, after reading six textbooks and passing three state exams, earned an Associate in Risk Management (ARM). In addition, I have passed two exams towards an Associate in Insurance Services (AIS) and plan on earning the designation early next year.

In August 2002, I joined the Toastmaster's Organization to develop better public speaking skills. As a member of the organization, I gave planned speeches and participated in impromptu debates. Toastmaster's is a great environment to improve because every speaker receives oral and written feedback from other members. Through my participation, I have won awards for Best Speaker, Best Speaker Evaluator, Best Debater and Best Table-Topics Speaker (A Table-Topic is a one-minute impromptu speech).

Being active in my church has also been an important part of my personal development. Last year, I taught workshops to help members of our congregation manage their personal finances. In the last nine years, I have led and managed over ten church play productions. It all started back in 1995 when John, our youth minister, was out of ideas of what to do for the Christmas production that year. On Sunday, he communicated the dilemma to our youth class and was open to any ideas we could offer. Historically, our plays have been good, however, they were always centered on the same Biblical themes. I suggested that we produce a play that applied the stories and principles of the Bible, but that took place during the present day, with present day problems and issues the audience could relate to. After presenting a premise for the production, John put me in charge of this production. Once I finished typing the script, I cast the production according to everyone's strengths and weaknesses. As the leader, I could not do everything myself; and so, I delegated tasks such as promotion, stage preparation and prop management. Over the next couple months of preparation, I learned how to lead and motivate a group. On Christmas Sunday, the production was so well received that our pastor appointed me as the head of future Easter and Christmas productions. The experience taught me that even at seventeen years old, I could step up, take charge and be listened to. This is a lesson I have ingrained into our current group of teenagers, who are planning to take the initiative and transition into a leadership role I accepted nine years ago. I am very proud of the legacy we have created.

Taking an active role in my professional and personal development has been an integral part of my success in life. Success is about using failure and life's setbacks as opportunities to learn, grow and become a stronger person as a result. Initially, college was a very frustrating experience. Although I could handle the coursework, the environment around me made it difficult to focus on my studies. However, while working part-time, sometimes up to thirty-five hours per week, I started making the dean's list and was eventually inducted into Beta Gamma Sigma.

A truly successful person has used their experiences to help others achieve success. This is a motto I live by, and perhaps the primary reason why I mentor others. I believe that if I had a close mentor before and during college, my college experience would have been much more fulfilling. Many things I had to learn on my own. However, I learned immensely from my experiences, and use them as a tool to mentor and advise current students and those planning to attend college. As someone who is first-generation corporate world, I learned a lot through research and trail and error. Everything, from how to research companies, interview and network, to the nuances of corporate culture, I learned through experience and by studying and asking questions. Now that I am knowledgeable in this area, I use that knowledge to advise college seniors and recent college grads on topics such as resume writing, interview skills and corporate "do's and don'ts. "

At my church there are youths with goals of attending college and working in the business world someday. Most of them are without mentors to guide them throughout the process of applying to colleges and choosing a major and career. For the high school students interested in business careers, I conducted a small workshop for them. The content of the workshop included the different concentrations within the business administration degree and the different career paths within business, from accounting to consulting. It also provided the students with an overview of how to keep up with business trends and how to land an internship in college and turn it into a full-time position. The workshop was a success, and the students verbalized their gratitude to me for conducting it. When I speak to them now, it is apparent that their goals and objectives are more focused. Currently, I am working on another workshop to follow up on their current questions and concerns. I know that after obtaining an MBA, I will have even more to offer others in the way of knowledge, experience and contacts. The more I learn and achieve, the more I have to give.

What are your short-term and long-term career aspirations? How will an MBA education further your development? Why does the academic experience offered at this school appeal to you?

The two major sides of our business are the client side and the broking side. I began my career at Marsh in fast-track program, acquiring technical knowledge in risk management, insurance principles, corporate finance and consultative selling, while working on client accounts. Through working on client accounts for two years, I acquired working knowledge of a variety of industries, from manufacturing and real estate to HVAC (heating, ventilation and air conditioning) and retail. With a solid foundation in client service and consulting, I fulfilled the role of a "trusted business advisor." Prior to business school, I will also have a year's experience on the broking side of our business, working and negotiating with insurance companies in order to obtain carrier placements for large commercial accounts. As a broker, I work on a greater number of client accounts and have become familiar with more industries.

Fall 2005 is a great time in my career to begin an MBA program. I will have just finished learning the broking-side of our business and will be ready to acquire more skills. My goal is to become a well-rounded leader and business advisor with an excellent foundation in many areas. This is why [School] is a good fit for me. [School]'s general management curriculum gives its students the freedom to take courses commensurate with their interests and long-term career goals without having to specialize in any given discipline. I am particularly interested in the areas of finance, strategy and entrepreneurship. An MBA in combination with my professional background will prepare me to become a more effective consultant, entrepreneur and business leader. I plan to take that knowledge and experience to work with not only start-up and growing companies but with growing economies as well. Although there are many opportunities within the United States, there are many more opportunities overseas for new and expanding industries. When I visited [School], it was exciting to see that other students shared the same interest of starting businesses overseas. Classmates are not only potential friends, but also potential business partners and contacts as well.

In October 2004, I attended a Minority Information Session in El Segundo, CA, where I met admissions representatives and recent alumni from the [School]. Then in November 2004, I was invited to participate in the "Many Voices: Perspectives on Diversity" event hosted by the school. The event was a great opportunity to learn more about the culture, atmosphere and student life at the [School].

Through the Many Voices event I learned a lot about the program, and it now appeals to me for a number of reasons. Business school is an opportunity to learn to become an effective leader and team player- two qualities [School] proactively develops in its students. These qualities were evident in the students I interacted with during my stay on the campus. Students I met were willing to take the time to provide insight on life at [School]- despite their grueling schedules. One student talked about his struggle during his first year due to his non-technical background, and about how his classmates pulled together to help him get his grades up. Another talked about how some students type up study notes and share them with their classmates. That astonished me because I formerly believed the business school environment to be highly competitive and individualistic. The panels during the conference were helpful in describing the culture of the school and the general attitudes of the students. Their candidness was insightful and appreciated. Because of the small student population, the environment at [School] seems to be very intimate and the level of camaraderie among students impressed me.

Business school is also an opportunity to not only acquire more business knowledge, but to take those tools and apply them. The Center for Entrepreneurial Studies is exciting, because it provides students with additional tools and opportunities to get involved with entrepreneurs in the community. The program is a great opportunity for students to pursue entrepreneurial opportunities that offer great opportunities but a low compensation. This is important, particularly because of my interest in consulting and entrepreneurship. At the [School], I plan to work on projects that will develop both skill sets. An MBA will be valuable to start-up and growing companies and economies. There are many opportunities worldwide for consultants and entrepreneurs, and [School]'s Global Management Immersion Experience enables students to apply their knowledge in different parts of the world.

At [School], I met many students from different backgrounds, from consulting to finance. However, no students I met were from my industry. Aside from my ethnicity, I can bring another element of diversity to the classroom. As a professional trained to analyze and manage risk for a wide array of clients, I will bring a different perspective to the dynamic classroom environment. Because of my uncommon background, I have a lot to offer to my classmates. Many business undergraduates, who typically lust after the management consulting and investment banking positions, often overlook the insurance industry. However, because risk is inherent in every business decision, it is important for leaders in an organization to understand how to identify, quantify and manage risk. Knowledge of the insurance markets is necessary for risks that must be transferred to a third party-a factor especially important for uncommon exposures. This is my background and is something unique that my classmates can learn from me.

Another unique quality that I can bring to [School] is that I have learned leadership skills from inside and outside of the office. From within the office, I have managed clients, projects and teams with great success. In addition, I have maintained ongoing relationships with numerous clients, advised them on their businesses and have managed colleagues to accomplish the surrounding tasks. Outside of the office, I have led and managed over ten church play productions, put together financial workshops to help people better manage their finances and helped some of my peers become better public speakers through the Toastmaster's Organization. Leadership does not begin and end at the workplace, but should encompass every aspect of life.

Please discuss your post-MBA short- and long-term professional goals. How will your professional experience, when combined with an MBA degree, allow you to achieve your goals?

The two major sides of our business are the client side and the broking side. I began my career at Marsh in a fast-track program, acquiring technical knowledge in risk management, insurance principles, corporate finance and consultative selling, while working on client accounts. Through working on client accounts for two years, I gained working knowledge of a variety of industries, from manufacturing and real estate to HVAC (heating, ventilation and air conditioning) and retail. With a solid foundation in client service and consulting, I fulfilled the role of a "trusted business advisor." Prior to starting graduate school, I will also have a year's experience on the broking side of our business, working and negotiating with insurance companies to obtain carrier placements for large commercial accounts. As a broker, I work on a greater number of client accounts and have become familiar with more industries.

Fall 2005 is a great time in my career to begin an MBA program. I will just have finished learning the broking side of our business and will be ready to learn more skills. My goal is to become a well-rounded leader and business advisor with an excellent foundation in many areas. This is why a general management curriculum is a good fit for me. A school with a general management curriculum gives its students the freedom to take advantage of a variety of courses without having to specialize in any given discipline. This will enable me to take courses commensurate with my interests and long-term career goals. I am particularly interested in the areas of finance, strategy and entrepreneurship, and plan to participate in field-based learning to apply the skills acquired in the classroom.

An MBA in combination with my professional background will prepare me to become a more effective consultant, entrepreneur and business leader. I plan to take that knowledge and experience and work with not only start-up and growing companies but with growing economies as well. Although there are many opportunities within the United States, there are even more opportunities overseas for trained business leaders. After talking to current MBA students, I was excited to learn that many students share the same interest of starting businesses overseas. Other students are not only potential friends, but potential business partners and contacts as well.

Describe a significant professional accomplishment that demonstrates your potential for a successful management career.

During my first year at Marsh, I recognized a need within the company. Although the company had a structured training program in place for Graduates, (the participants in an intensive one-year program) no formalized orientation program existed for new employees. As a result, most new employees were ignorant of the roles of other sister companies and departments, technical resources within the organization, job functions of other colleagues and the criteria for promotion within the organization.

After interviewing members of our senior management to find out the information they thought was important for new hires to know, I compiled the results of my research and presented a solution. I proposed to senior management that we do two things. First, that we put together a written guide containing information important to new employees. Second, that we conduct mini-seminars, perhaps during lunchtime, where department managers educate new employees about the roles and functions of their departments. Management liked the idea and put me in charge of the project.

The guide would give an overview of the organization and the different departments, licensing and designation requirements, client team roles and technological resources available to colleagues. Because of the size of the task, I delegated the copying and assembling to other colleagues. Once the fifty-five-page book was completed, our Human Resources department gave it to new employees and used it as a template for the western region of the firm.

Along with the written guide, I initiated informational workshops for newer employees. During each workshop, a department manager talked about the roles and functions of his department and opened up a question and answer session. The workshops were successful at educating newer employees about other areas of the company.

This was one of the first projects at Marsh that I managed from start to finish. I saw a need within the organization, and then proposed and implemented the solution. The success of this project taught me that although I was new to the company, I could take a leadership role in a project and make a valuable contribution. When I become a manager, I will expect the same initiative from all employees, old and new.

What have you done in your business, personal, or academic life to demonstrate commitment to the Consortium's mission? *(The mission of the Consortium for Graduate Study in Management is to encourage and enable the largest possible number of the best and the brightest African American, Hispanic American and Native*

American college graduates to pursue successful careers in management.)

Success is using failure and life's setbacks as opportunities to learn, grow and become a stronger person as a result. A truly successful person is one who has used those experiences to help others achieve success as well. This is a motto I live by, and perhaps the primary reason why I mentor others. I believe that if I had a close mentor before and during college, my college experience would have been much more fulfilling. At my church are minority youths with goals of attending college and working in the business world someday. Most of them are without mentors to guide them throughout the process of applying to colleges and choosing a major and career.

Many things I had to learn on my own through trial and error. However, I learned immensely from my experiences, and use them as a tool to mentor and advise current students and those planning to attend college. As someone who is first-generation corporate world, I had to learn many aspects of it through research and trail and error. Everything, from how to research companies, interview and network, to the nuances of corporate culture, I learned through experience, study and by asking questions. Now that I am much more knowledgeable in this area, I use that knowledge to advise college seniors and recent college grads on topics such as resume writing, interview skills and corporate do's and don'ts. For the high school and college students at church interested in a career in business, I conducted a small workshop to introduce them to the different ways to start their business careers. Through the workshop, I touched on a variety of topics, including the different concentrations within the Business Administration major and the different career paths in business, from accounting to consulting. It also provided the students with an overview of how to keep up with business trends and how to land an internship in college and turn it into a full-time position. The workshop was a success, and the students verbalized their gratitude to me for conducting it. When I speak to them now, it is apparent that their goals and objectives are much more focused. Currently, I am working on another workshop to follow up on their current questions and concerns. I know that after obtaining an MBA, I will have even more to offer others in the way of knowledge, experience and contacts. The more I learn and achieve, the more I have to give.

Talk about a leadership role you had early in life.

Since I can remember, my church has put on plays every Easter and Christmas. Usually, a few adult teachers would collaborate and write a play to be performed, and then cast the teenagers as actors. Each teacher would then have a role in the management of the entire production, which included rehearsals, costumes, props, stage design and promotion.

Back in 1995, John, our youth minister, was out of ideas of what to do for the Christmas production that year. On Sunday, he communicated the dilemma to our youth class and was open to any ideas we could offer. Historically, our plays have been good, however, they were always centered on the same themes. Easter plays were always about the resurrection of Christ and were set during Biblical times. Christmas plays were always about the birth of Jesus, and always included characters like Mary and the three wise men. I raised my hand and suggested that we produce a play that applied the stories and principles of the Bible, but that took place in the present day, with present day problems and issues the audience could relate to. I presented a premise for the production that John and my peers responded favorably to. And so, at the age of seventeen, I was put in charge of this production and got to work on the script.

Once I finished the script, the production was ready to be cast. I had a feel for everyone's strengths and weaknesses, and so, I cast the production accordingly. Some members of our class were assigned leading roles, some supporting roles, and some non-speaking roles. Although I was in charge, I could not do everything myself; and so, I delegated tasks such as promotion, stage preparation and props management. Over the next couple months of preparation, I learned how to lead and motivate a group and delegate tasks to the right people, while acquiring management and organizational skills.

On Christmas Sunday it was show time, and our months of hard work would come down to our performance on this day. The pressure was on and our team executed well under my leadership. The production was so well received that I was appointed to be in charge of future Easter and Christmas productions. The subject matter was radically different from that of past plays, and the quality of the script, dialogue and set were a dramatic step up from prior years. From that point on, our team was held to a much higher standard.

The experience taught me that although I was very young at the time, I could step up, take charge and be listened to. This is a lesson I have ingrained into our current group of teenagers, who are planning to take the initiative and transition into a leadership role I accepted nine years ago. I am very proud of the legacy we have created.

Describe the steps you proactively took to develop professionally and personally over the past two years.

When I began the search for a career after college, I wanted to work in an environment that would develop my technical, professional and communication skills. After extensive research, Marsh's Graduate Training Program seemed like the type of program that would accomplish this. It is a highly selective, rigorous program designed to accelerate its colleagues' integration into Marsh and make them productive more quickly by supplementing skills learned on the job with formal training in insurance, risk management, accounting, financial analysis and professional skills. It was a great opportunity and I applied to the program. After passing a series of interviews and a one-hour case, I was accepted into the one-year program.

Since the program, I have continued to take steps to develop my technical and professional skills. In June 2004,

I successfully self-studied for and earned an Associate in Risk Management (ARM), a professional designation requiring the completion of six textbooks and the passing of three state exams. In addition, I have passed two exams towards an Associate in Insurance Services (AIS) and plan on earning the designation early next year.

In August 2002, I joined the Toastmaster's Organization to develop better public speaking skills. As a member of the organization, I gave planned and impromptu speeches and participated in impromptu debates. Toastmaster's is a great environment to improve your skills because every speaker receives oral and written feedback from other members. Through my participation, I have won awards for Best Speaker, Best Evaluator, Best Debater and Best Table-Topics Speaker (A Table-Topic is a one-minute impromptu speech).

Staying involved with the community has also been an important part of my personal development. By sharing my time and experiences with others I have acquired professional skills while giving back to the community. Outside of the office, I have led and managed over ten church play productions, conducted free workshops to help people better manage their personal finances and mentored high school and college students.

Describe how you will approach co-creating your MBA: What career goals have you set and what objectives will you establish for your MBA experience? How will you utilize the opportunities to achieve your objectives and

***create an MBA experience that is right for you? How will
you and your approach benefit other members of our
community?***

Generally speaking, I was looking for a prestigious
program with a solid general management curriculum.
After researching numerous business programs, [School]
caught my attention. In addition, every profile I read on
[School] highlighted the communal atmosphere of the
program. After further research, I visited the website for
more detailed information on the curriculum, academic
programs and student life.

A [School] MBA appeals to me for many reasons.
Business school is an opportunity to learn to become an
effective leader and team player- two qualities [School]
proactively develops in its students. In addition, with the
small student population, the environment at [School]
seems to be intimate, with a high level of camaraderie
among its students.

Business school is also an opportunity to not only
acquire more business knowledge, but to take those tools
and apply them. The Multidisciplinary Action Project is
exciting, because it gives [School] students the opportunity
to work on projects for real clients or to develop their own
entrepreneurial ideas. This is important because of my
interest in consulting and entrepreneurship. The
Multidisciplinary Action Project will give me a chance to
work on projects that will develop both skill sets. I have an
interest in working with not only global firms but with

start-up and growing enterprises as well. There are many opportunities nationwide for consultants and entrepreneurs, and [School]'s Multidisciplinary Action Project enables students to apply their knowledge in different parts of the country. Through this program, my goal is to earn a leadership role in the launch of a new enterprise.

Aside from my ethnicity, I can bring another element of diversity to the classroom. As a professional trained to analyze and manage risk for a wide array of clients, I will bring another perspective to the dynamic classroom environment. Because of my uncommon background, I will have a lot to offer to my classmates. Many business undergraduates, who typically lust after the management consulting and investment banking positions, often overlook the insurance industry. However, because risk is inherent in every business decision, it is important for leaders in an organization to understand how to identify, quantify and manage risk. Knowledge of the insurance markets is necessary for risks that must be transferred to a third party- a factor especially important for uncommon exposures. My background will make me an asset not only to my classmates and study groups, but also to my project teammates during the Multidisciplinary Action Project.

Why is [School] the best MBA program for you?

Generally speaking, I was looking for a prestigious program with a solid general management curriculum. After researching numerous business programs, [School] caught my attention. In addition, every profile I read on [School] highlighted the communal atmosphere of the program. After further research, I visited the website for more detailed information on the curriculum, academic programs and student life. It was there that I learned of the [School] Diversity Conference.

The Conference seemed like a great opportunity to not only learn more about [School], but to experience it as well. It was also important to determine whether I was a good fit for the culture of the school. This is a factor that cannot be ascertained online, or by reading U.S. News or any other publication. The number of business school applicants I speak to who do not make the effort to visit any of the schools they apply to shocks me. Thankfully, [School] extended an invitation to me to participate in the Conference.

Through the Conference I learned a lot about the program, and it now appeals to me for a number of reasons. Business school is an opportunity to learn to become an effective leader and team player- two qualities [School] proactively develops in its students. These are qualities I saw in the students I interacted with during my stay at [School], from [student name], my hospitable student host who made me feel at home at his dorm in Whittemore Hall, to the students who were willing to take the time to provide insight on life at [School]- despite their grueling schedules. With the small student population, the environment at [School] seems to be very intimate and the level of camaraderie among students impressed me.

Business school is also an opportunity to not only acquire more business knowledge, but to take those tools and apply them. The Leadership Forum is exciting, because it gives [School] students the opportunity to work on projects for real clients or to develop their own entrepreneurial ideas. This was key for me, particularly because I am interested in consulting and entrepreneurship, and I see business school as a venue to work on projects that will develop both skill sets. My plan is to work with not only start-up and growing companies, but with growing economies as well. While at [School], I met students interested in starting business overseas. [Student name], a second-year [School] student, learned of my interest in international business from another prospective student and made an effort to find me. [Student name] told me about the two businesses he started in Trinidad and Tobago, and about the opportunities at [School] for students interested in entrepreneurial opportunities overseas. There are many opportunities worldwide for consultants and entrepreneurs, and [School]'s Field Study in International Business enables students to apply their knowledge in different parts of the world.

At [School] I met many students from different backgrounds, from consulting to finance. However, no students I met at [School] were from my industry. Aside from my ethnicity, I can bring another element of diversity to [School]. As a professional trained to analyze and manage risk for a wide array of clients, I will bring another perspective to the dynamic classroom environment. Because of my uncommon background, I will have a lot to offer to my classmates. Many business undergraduates, who typically lust after the management consulting and investment banking positions, often overlook the insurance industry. However, because risk is inherent in every business decision, it is important for leaders in an organization to understand how to identify, quantify and manage risk. Knowledge of the insurance markets is necessary for risks that must be transferred to a third party- a factor especially important for uncommon exposures. This is my background and is something unique that my classmates can learn from me.

Why is [School] the perfect fit for your MBA?

A [School] MBA appeals to me for many reasons. Generally speaking, I was looking for a prestigious program with a solid general management curriculum. After researching numerous business programs, [School] caught my attention. The curriculum provides a general management foundation without the requirement to specialize in any given area. However, students have the option of choosing a specialization commensurate with their interests, or can simply take classes in line with their career goals.

Business school is an opportunity to acquire more business knowledge and to take those tools and apply them. An MBA in combination with my professional background will prepare me to become a more effective consultant, entrepreneur and business leader. I plan to take that knowledge and experience and work with not only start-up and growing companies but with growing economies as well. Although there are many opportunities within the United States, even more opportunities exist overseas for trained business leaders. [School]'s International Management Program enables students to apply their knowledge in different parts of the world.

What I like most is the [School] Incubator. The [School] Incubator is exciting, because it gives students the opportunity to develop their own entrepreneurial ideas. This is important because of my interest in entrepreneurship. My dream is to launch an enterprise as a business student, and this program provides each student with that opportunity. Through this program, my goal is to collaborate with other students and develop a business idea to submit to the [School] Incubator.

If the idea is not accepted, I plan to search for entrepreneurial and internship opportunities in the city. Another great feature of [School] is its downtown location, providing students with access to numerous corporations and business opportunities. I plan to network and seek opportunities with start-up or growing enterprises in the Manhattan area. My background in insurance and risk consulting, combined with my MBA, will make me an asset to many growing corporations.

Aside from my ethnicity, I can bring another element of diversity to the classroom. As a professional trained to analyze and manage risk for a wide array of clients, I will bring another perspective to the dynamic classroom environment. Because of my uncommon background, I will have a lot to offer to my classmates. Many business undergraduates, who typically lust after the management consulting and investment banking positions, often overlook the insurance industry. However, because risk is inherent in every business decision, it is important for leaders in an organization to understand how to identify, quantify and manage risk. Knowledge of the insurance markets is necessary for risks that must be transferred to a third party- a factor especially important for uncommon exposures. My background will make me an asset to my classmates and study groups.

10

I'VE SUBMITTED MY APPLICATIONS. NOW WHAT?

Once you've submitted all of your applications, you can pat yourself on the back and rest easy for a bit, but not for too long. In the interim, make sure to do the following:

- **Pay attention to the financial aid requirements of each school.** Every school has its own financial aid policy. If you plan on applying for aid, you must complete the FAFSA (http://www.fafsa.ed.gov/) by March 1st of the year you will be entering business school. Additionally, some schools provide a link to their financial aid applications once a student is admitted. Others have their own forms for you to complete even before you are notified of admission, so be on the look out. Visit each school's website and pay attention to its financial aid timeline.

- **Brush up on your interview skills.** Especially if you haven't interviewed in a while, it's not a bad idea to practice your responses to common interview questions. Typically, the questions will be somewhat similar to the ones you answered in completing the application. So review your essay responses and practice verbalizing the points you want to make.

www.ingramcontent.com/pod-product-compliance
Lightning Source LLC
Chambersburg PA
CBHW022123170526
45157CB00004B/1729